© Copyright 2015 by J. Victor McGuire

All rights reserved. Printed in the United States of America. Except as permitted under the United States Copyright Act of 1976, no part of this publication may be reproduced or distributed in any form or by any means, or stored in a data base retrieval system, without prior written permission of the publisher.

Library of Congress Cataloging Publication Data
Library of Congress Catalog card number: 89-91959

ISBN: 978-0692463482

3RD
EDITION

A TEEN GUIDE TO LEADERSHIP AND SERVICE

WRITTEN BY J. VICTOR MCGUIRE, PH.D.

A TEEN GUIDE TO LEADERSHIP AND SERVICE

Featuring:

What is Leadership?

The Best Way to Get into College

Career Development

Self-Esteem

Service Learning

Motivation

Communication

Health

Literacy

Time Management

Mentoring

Pre-college Counseling

Coping with Stress

ACKNOWLEDGEMENTS

Thank you to my wife Susan McGuire
who loves and supports me like no other.

Over the years there have been multitudes
of friends, parents, colleagues and administrators
who have shared my enthusiasm to activate
the potential of our youth.
I am eternally grateful for all of you.
Keep moving our youth forward.

I would like to thank Annie H. and her friends,
Jocelyn C., Susan T., Matt W., Javin D.,
for making the cover come to life.

FOREWORD

I hope everyone who reads this book will have a chance someday to meet its author, J. Victor McGuire. Victor is that special kind of person who immediately engages you, enjoys being with you, and makes you feel the world is a better place because you are part of it.

This book will never replace an opportunity to meet Victor up close and personal, but it is a superb opportunity for every young person facing the challenges of growing up to experience Victor's beliefs about life, school, and young people. The book will take you through the steps necessary to confirm that you are a special person and that life is better when there are "no negatives." Victor is a master teacher, and this book is his masterpiece!

Victor believes that the most important ideals you have are those ideals you have about yourself. He knows the importance of school and the academic side of life, and he is also committed to sharing with young people the strategies to help make them more effective human beings. Victor knows how important self-esteem, motivation, communication and community involvement are to you and he has put together in this wonderful book a series of activities that will help you in each of these areas. This is not a "textbook" in the usual sense, but in some ways it is a "course," teaching how to deal with the ups and downs, the joys and disappointments, and the challenges of growing up in a complex but exciting world.

The greatest thing about reading this book will be that you won't just be able to read it; you are going to want to go out and DO this book. It will help you to see the value in yourself and the people around you; it will help you feel better about the problems you face everyday. In many ways, it is likely to become a companion, a treasury of ideas to help you become all you are capable of becoming.

Victor often talks about life being a journey with you in the driver's seat. In this book he has provided a road map that will make the journey just a little more exciting, a little more rewarding, and a little more fun.

I know you are going to like this book. It may be the most important book you ever read, but if it is not, at least you will have had an opportunity to spend time with the thoughts and suggestions of one of the most important educators of our time, and then I hope you get to meet Victor some day in person. He will change your life. He has helped to change mine.

Tomas R. Giblin, Ph.D.
Professor of Education/Department Chair
The College of Brockport
State University of New York

TABLE OF CONTENTS

WELCOME TO THE THIRD EDITION OF THE
NO NEGATIVES LEADERSHIP GUIDE!

MY HOPE FOR THE BOOK IS UNCHANGED FROM EARLIER EDITIONS: to provide middle school students real tools with practical value to develop leadership skills and empower them throughout their lives.

Building upon that, I'm tremendously enthused about the new material we've added to this edition – a new chapter with terrific information for you and your parents. Insightful college-planning strategies and great tips from a notable high school counselor and admissions officer at a top university. Not only is it not too early, today it's more important than ever to begin planning for college in middle school.

No Negatives is a book that doesn't just talk at you but encourages you to participate. Doing so develops skills enabling you to proactively redefine your future by understanding what leadership is really all about, and why it matters. You'll learn what you can do starting today to become the best you can be.

You'll have fun with this book and discover that infinitely more attention is paid to what you can do, rather than what you can't or shouldn't do. It's a book about possibilities that I truly believe are limitless...if you begin today by approaching every day with the right attitude.

I want you to know that I have a special feeling for all of this and I'm not simply talking at you with big ideas in a vacuum. It's a far more personal and heartfelt mission that motivates me. Here's what I mean by that.

This book is about recognizing two things that are critical life choices:

FIRST, MIDDLE SCHOOL REALLY IS AN INCREDIBLY IMPORTANT TIME IN YOUR LIFE.

I loved middle school. I truly did.

Decisions made now, or not, and good habits adopted now, or not, can propel you to new heights and great accomplishments. It's up to you.

AND SECOND, THE RIGHT ATTITUDE AND MINDSET ARE REMARKABLY POWERFUL TOOLS YOU CAN USE TO OPEN DOORS FOR YOU THE REST OF LIFE. But ignoring them can hamper you for the rest of your life. Making the right choices matters.

These are big decisions, no doubt about that, but they are truly worthy ones. After all, life is a great adventure and the future really is what we make of it. Your choices and habits will make all the difference.

HOW DO I KNOW? I'M LIVING PROOF OF IT.

I was born in Chicago. But I grew up in a boys' school. As a young African-American boy, I was shuttled between caregivers and stepmothers. I was placed and displaced. At the age of 12, I was packed off to a school for troubled youth. I really didn't know if this was good or not, but it felt okay.

It would be fair to say I was one of those kids without much of a chance, and was most likely destined to be lost and chewed up by a system that didn't care about me. But life is what we make of it. For me it was all about opportunity.

I discovered sports – basketball and track – and while loving and excelling at each was nice, the values of teamwork and dedication – working hard and never giving up – changed me fundamentally.

School eventually became important, and I dedicated myself to learning with the support of some good mentors. I adopted better habits and earned the chance to attend college. I had zero college counseling. I just recognized others were going, so why not me?

I went to college, graduated and joined an international educational organization. Education had become a part of my life and from then on, always would be.

I became a teacher and have dedicated my life to it, teaching at the middle school, high school and college levels across the country and at private schools around the world. I've even had the privilege of founding an association for beginning teachers, to help them and give back.

I earned a Master's degree and later, my Doctorate in Education.

I was awarded a Fulbright Scholarship in South Africa and met Winnie Mandela and Bishop Desmond Tutu. Imagine that student from Chicago meeting two of the most inspirational leaders in the world!

WHAT'S TRUE IS THAT LIFE IS FULL OF TEACHABLE MOMENTS THAT, IF WE CHOOSE TO TAKE ADVANTAGE OF THEM, ENRICH AND INSPIRE US. My hope is that this book will do a little of both for you by arming you with skills to make better choices, empowering you to believe in yourself, and instilling confidence that you can do whatever you set your mind and heart on.

WHAT YOU MAKE OF YOUR LIFE REALLY IS UP TO YOU.

THE QUESTION IS WHICH PATH WILL YOU TAKE?

Will you be admired and successful, remembered for taking full advantage of your many leadership opportunities and making the most of them?

Or, will you be remembered as someone who, sadly, had great potential but never took advantage of it and suffered because of it?

Make the right choices, develop good habits, and everything is possible. Dream big and never stop, but adopt the positive attitude and mindset to make your dreams come true.

You really can, and it starts today with a book that's about you, not me.

Good luck and have fun with it!

J. Victor McGuire, Ph.D.

WHAT IS

LEADERSHIP?

Leadership can be explained in a variety of different ways.

1. Leadership is a way of influencing an individual or group to attain a set of goals by effective communication.

2. Leadership is the ability to inspire, enlighten, and provide vision to a group of people as they work to achieve agreed-upon goals.

3. Leadership is a key component that motivates and organizes a group or an individual to accomplish their objectives.

4. Leadership is a way of getting your peers to go farther and do more than what is simply expected. For example, a leader would be able to get a group of people together for the planning of a special school or community activity.

5. Leadership is an act that can possibly cause your peers to act in a positive manner. This would be leadership by example.

A true leader can persuade in a positive way, influence and inspire, and be a motivating factor to help get things done. As a leader, you will help create a vision for others and assist them in achieving it. You will need a group of peers that are **confident** – in you. And once this happens, they will give you their support.

So now do you have a better idea of what leadership means?

SO WHY SHOULD YOU BE A LEADER?

One of the big advantages of being a leader is that it gives you a feeling of accomplishment. People admire leaders and with that comes **prestige.** By being a leader you will be in position to help others and will be making others successful. In turn that will help you feel better about yourself.

If you begin the journey of putting yourself in a leadership position now, it will have big payoffs in the future. In the work world, leadership positions pay well; top corporate leaders can earn as much as 150 times as much as entry-level workers. This isn't to say you should be **motivated** entirely by money, but it is something to consider.

CAN YOU PERSUADE, MOTIVATE AND INSPIRE?

These are some of the basic areas of leadership: how and what you do – or will – accomplish by incorporating these qualities.

Persuasion is a way to get your peers to change their course of thinking and to begin to consider another way of doing something that they had not previously considered.

Inspiration is possibly the highest form of leadership, because here you are motivating others based on your positive personality.

Motivation is the hardest part about being a leader. This requires the skill of getting someone to go farther, and do more as they put more into the task at hand. Motivation is truly the nuts and bolts of being a leader.

LEADERS THINK ABOUT THE BIG PICTURE

1. Leaders think about how they can make a situation better.

2. Leaders are willing to take positive risks.

3. Leaders form positive relationships with their peers.

4. Leaders help build their environment and schools into better places.

5. Leaders are always looking to improve themselves.

DO THESE STATEMENTS SOUND FAMILIAR?

- Nobody asks my opinion.
- I may not be right about this but.
- I might not be as smart as others.

Statements like these do nothing except preserve low self confidence.

Negative self-talk damages your self-confidence and your ability to lead. Ideally you want to look at your weaknesses for ways you can improve, but positive thinking yields positive results.

Leadership points to consider:

- Dive in. Get experience in the areas you're interested in.

- Stay tuned-in. Read, investigate, and learn from others.

- Learn to listen. Listening and observing peers is a great way to learn.

- Stay committed to your leadership goals.

- Ask questions about your interests.

- Keep a journal about your leadership goals.

THE BEST WAY TO GET INTO

COLLEGE

A college education is a major factor in achieving success in the world today. Getting a college education requires time, effort, and planning by you and your parents. Working together, you'll reach this important goal.

A TWO- OR FOUR-YEAR COLLEGE DEGREE IS BECOMING **MORE AND MORE IMPORTANT** AS THE KEY TO UNLOCKING THE DOORS TO ECONOMIC ADVANCEMENT.

A college education will help you acquire a wide range of knowledge in many subjects. College also teaches students to express their thoughts clearly in speech and in writing, to make informed decisions, and to use technology to their best advantage.

A college education builds on the knowledge and skills acquired in earlier years. It's best to begin thinking about your high school course schedule in seventh or eighth grade. Students that don't plan ahead may not complete the required or recommended courses that help them qualify for and remain in college.

If you are in middle school/junior high get on a college preparatory path right away. The U. S. Department of

Education recommends that middle and junior high school students take Algebra I in eighth grade, geometry in ninth grade, and English, science, and history or geography every year. It is very important that you continue to take math classes as a high school senior, so you are prepared for college math. Yes, math needs to be your friend, not your enemy!

Foreign language, computer, and visual or performing art classes are also recommended. If you are struggling in math, English, or reading, get help from a tutor or your teacher. If you don't ask, you won't receive it.

IF YOU ARE IN SIXTH GRADE, YOU SHOULD BE DOING THE FOLLOWING THINGS:

- Start to adopt good study habits.
- Sit down with your parents and chart the path leading you to college.
- Challenge yourself academically and get involved in school activities.
- Meet with your counselor to learn what college preparatory classes are offered.
- Attend any college information day programs at your school or in your area to find out about colleges near you.

IF YOU ARE IN THE SEVENTH GRADE:

- Keep your grades up, with special effort in math and English.
- Meet regularly with your school counselor.
- Discuss career and college options with your parents.
- Aim high and explore all options.
- Start on a college preparatory track now!

- Take the courses you need to be successful in high school.
- If you need a tutor, find one!

IF YOU ARE IN THE EIGHTH GRADE:

- If you haven't already taken Algebra I, now is the time.
- Go online and explore the many informational college and career resources available.
- Your parents should begin thinking about how they are going to finance college.
- It's never too early to start your savings plan.

IF YOU ARE IN NINTH GRADE:

- This is when it all begins to count, so get off to a solid start with your grades and maintain a strong grade point average (GPA).
- Sit down with your parents to develop a plan of courses you will need to graduate and be eligible for college admission.
- Begin to look at SAT and ACT test dates.
- Learn about any state scholarships that may be available to you based on how you do in high school.
- Begin to get familiar with the college admissions process.
- Make sure you are taking the right course work.
- Look at the opportunities offered at community college courses for high school students and discuss them with your parents. Some states will allow you to take course work during your junior/senior year that will count for college course work.

IF YOU ARE IN TENTH GRADE:

- Your Academic Student Planner should be updated to include completed ninth grade classes and upcoming tenth grade classes.

- Meet with your high school counselor to ensure you're on track.

- Sign up for the PSAT (Preliminary Scholastic Assessment Test) to help prepare for the SAT (Scholastic Assessment Test) in high school.

- Consider taking AP (Advanced Placement) classes.

- Make sure you are prepared for any state proficiency exams you may be required to take in order to receive your high school diploma.

- As your college fund continues to grow, begin to investigate federal, state, and private financial aid.

- Check to see if your school offers the Preliminary Scholastic Assessment Test/National Merit Scholarship Qualifying Test. PSAT/NMSQT is a practice test to prepare you for the Scholastic Assessment Test (SAT). Students that do well on this test, and meet other academic performance criteria, may qualify for the National Merit Scholarship Program.

- Visit local college campuses, take visitor tours, and ask the guides about their college experiences.

- Your course work should include Algebra II, English, and a foreign language.

- Begin to do Internet research and make a list of colleges you would like to attend. Begin investigating cost, distance from home, and curriculum.

IF YOU ARE IN THE ELEVENTH GRADE:

- Your course work should include advanced math and English.

- Look into taking AP classes.

- You should now have a good idea of which c olleges are on your wish list.

- Your counselor will help you decide when to take the ACT or SAT college entrance exams. Registering for exams is usually one month in advance.

- Results from exams taken in the spring or summer arrive in time to retake the test in the fall of your senior year, if necessary.

- Add test scores to your student planner.

- Prepare for the SAT or ACT by reviewing books with testing tips; make vocabulary cards.

- Attend college fairs and sessions with college representatives.

- By now you should have your Social Security number, which is required on most college and financial aid applications.

- Continue researching federal, state, and private scholarships by finding out what awards students in your school are receiving.

IF YOU ARE IN THE 12TH GRADE:

- Your college application process begins this year.
- Register for the ACT or SAT if you did not take the test last year or if you have decided to retake the test.
- Check college applications by early October.
- If you want to live on campus, and have not already done so, complete a housing/meal plan application.
- By December, begin researching all of the financial aid opportunities.
- Request that your high school send the transcripts of your first semester senior year grades to the colleges to which you've applied.
- Monitor your applications to make sure that all materials are sent and received on time. Review your Student Aid Report for accuracy.
- In April, review financial aid award letters with your parents and be sure you understand the terms and conditions for each type of aid offered.
- In May, work with your parents to establish a budget for your books, supplies, and living expenses.
- Determine how much of that budget grants and scholarships will cover, how much your parents will provide, and how much you will contribute by working and/or with student loans.
- Celebrate your acceptance to college – you've earned it!
- In June, request that your high school send a copy of your final transcripts to the colleges you want to attend.
- Find out when payment for tuition, room, board, etc. will be due.
- In July/August, pack and look forward to a stimulating and rewarding college experience!!!

DEVELOPMENT

JOBS YOU CAN GET WITH A COLLEGE EDUCATION

One of the major benefits of acquiring a college education is having more job options. Parents should talk with their children and ask about professions that interest them, and then obtain more information about those professions by consulting with the high school guidance office, local college advisory centers, or the Occupational Outlook handbook in your public library. Some professions require an advanced degree, such as medicine or law, beyond a traditional four-year degree. As you mature and learn more about requirements or different professions, you will be in a better position to make a degree program decision.

TWO-YEAR COLLEGE

Associate Degree

- Administrative Assistant
- Automotive Mechanic
- Commercial Technician
- Dental Hygienist
- Engineering Technician
- Heating, Air Conditioning and Refrigeration Technician
- Hotel/Restaurant Manager

- Medical Laboratory Technician
- Surveyor
- Water and Wastewater Treatment Plant Operator

FOUR-YEAR COLLEGE
Bachelor's Degree

- Accountant
- Dietician
- FBI Agent
- Insurance Agent
- Journalist
- Registered Nurse
- Teacher
- Computer Systems Analyst
- Engineer
- Graphic Designer
- Investment Banker
- Public Relations Specialist
- Social Worker
- Writer

MORE THAN FOUR YEARS
Graduate and Professional Degrees

- Architect
- Doctor
- Geologist
- Pharmacist
- Public Policy Analyst
- Scientist
- Veterinarian
- Dentist
- Economist
- Lawyer
- Priest or Rabbi
- Psychologist
- University Professor
- Zoologist

CAREER AWARENESS

Whether it's your first job or the next one that pays more than the last one, finding a job or deciding what you think you might want to do is a job in itself.

Are you aware of the fact that there are over 30,000 job titles?

If I gave you a sheet of paper and asked you to list as many jobs as you could, how many could you list? Twenty, fifty, a hundred?

Let's see how many job titles you can list right now:

_____   _____

_____   _____

_____   _____

_____   _____

_____   _____

_____   _____

_____   _____

_____   _____

_____   _____

_____   _____

_____   _____

_____   _____

_____   _____

_____   _____

_____   _____

_____   _____

_____   _____

HOW DID YOU DO?

Fifty, seventy-five, one hundred fifty? Not bad...but isn't it amazing to think that there are over 30,000 job titles? If you can only list fifty or so, look at what you could be missing out on. This information is very valuable.

As you begin to think about your future occupation, I'll give you a simple activity and an opportunity you'll find rewarding and informative. The activity is conducting an informational interview.

All you need to do is identify someone in a job you might be interested in. Contact him or her and set up an appointment and ask questions like these:

1. How did you get this job, or how did you become interested in this kind of work?

2. What do you like/dislike about your work?

3. What would you like to change about your job?

4. In your opinion, what are the problems in your field of work?

5. What are the most important skills you use?

6. How could you be more effective in your job?

7. If you were to change jobs, what would you like to do?

8. Who are two people who do similar work that I could talk to?

9. May I use your name?

Upon completion of your interview, ask for a business card or their address and send them a follow-up thank you note.

POSTIVE OUTCOMES OF CAREER DEVELOPMENT

- An improved attitude toward work will be invaluable in your life.

- A better understanding and appreciation of relationships between work and lifestyle patterns.

- An enhanced ability to communicate with adult workers.

- A more realistic understanding of how a business organization operates.

- An increased understanding of the private enterprise system.

- A better understanding of the variety of career paths followed by adult workers during their working life.

- An opportunity to see adult workers as role models for career decisions.

**"Life is not about finding yourself.
Life is about creating yourself."**

—Lolly Daskal

WHY
SELF-ESTEEM?

With positive self-esteem, you look and feel good and tend to be more effective and productive in your daily life. When you are feeling good about yourself, you tend to give some of those traits away to other people in a positive fashion.

Self-esteem affects everyone around us, especially our families. Imagine how harmonious your household would be if everyone felt confident and good about themselves! It can be contagious. Try it — you'll be amazed!

Although there are a great many positive things going on in today's world, unfortunately not enough of them are being recognized.

So as we journey through this book, we'll explore ways to better recognize and appreciate the positive things about ourselves and others. My hope is that it helps you use your resources to become the best YOU can be!

In this section I would like you to introduce yourself. I introduced myself to you, earlier, and now it's your turn. Describe yourself in three words.

1. _____

2. _____

3. _____

List five positive qualities about yourself.

1. _____

2. _____

3. _____

4. _____

5. _____

WHO ARE YOU?

Let's begin this section by taking a few minutes to evaluate who you are. Read through the following list of characteristics and rate yourself using the space provided below.

1=Never   2=Occasionally   3=Mostly   4=Always

_____   I feel secure about who I am.

_____   I like other people's company.

_____   I can make friends easily.

_____   I feel important.

_____   If I fail, I try and try again.

_____   I am honest in my feelings about other people.

_____   I am good at helping other people.

_____   I am special.

_____   I easily say "thank you" after someone pays
            me a compliment.

_____   I think of the idea first.

Getting to know yourself, and learning to accept yourself for who and what you are, is an essential step toward positive self-esteem. Look at your list; go back through all the characteristics that you marked with a three or four. These can be considered your strengths.

You should appreciate your strengths. Ones or twos are characteristics you may want to work to improve. Don't hesitate to ask a parent or teacher what you can do to improve your weaknesses.

> **"Just when the caterpillar thought the world was ending, he turned into a butterfly."**
>
> —Proverb

LEVELS OF SELF-ESTEEM

Now that you have established a better idea of who you are, let us take a look at three different levels of self-esteem. As we do, you'll begin to zero in on where you fit.

1. **People with high levels of self-esteem:**

   - Feel self-confident and believe in themselves.

   - Can take constructive criticism.

   - Are not threatened by failure.

   - Accept and appreciate situations and try not to criticize or complain.

   - Are most likely to be in good physical shape.

   - Are not critical of themselves to the point where they are constantly putting themselves down.

2. **With an intermediate level of self-esteem, you:**

- Are a cautious person.

- Look for others to assist in your decision-making process.

- Look for ways to please people.

This next level may be of no real concern for you, but you may know someone at this level and offer a few words of encouragement for them.

3. **People who experience low levels of self-esteem generally possess these characteristics:**

- Loners.

- Expect to fail.

- Would rather isolate themselves from a group than participate.

- Very sensitive to ridicule.

- They find a way to fail rather than looking for ways to succeed.

**"No one can make you feel inferior
without your consent."**

—Eleanor Roosevelt

NEXT, LET'S IMPLEMENT OR INCREASE YOUR POSITIVE SELF-ESTEEM. This can be achieved by working on your attitude. I realize we all have setbacks, but it's time for a fresh start and to believe you will only go up from here.

Before continuing with self-esteem, let's consider how society looks at us. Unfortunately, if we look at ourselves too much we are viewed as self-centered. So, before I ask you to take a look at yourself, I would like to share this story about a former seventh grade class of mine.

You decide the outcome of any situation by your attitude.

FASHION SHOW 101

One day when I was a seventh grade teacher, I happened to notice that a student was sporting some new clothes, so I made a comment that I liked them. Well, she did a double-take and decided to turn on her charm and become an instant fashion model. She started strutting her stuff, saying, "These pants are from The Limited, and the shoes are from Nike."

Well, the whole class was cracking up! This particular student felt pretty good about herself, but she also had a great ability as a seventh grader to create an environment to allow others to feel good about themselves. So I got to thinking about our impromptu fashion show. I wondered, Wouldn't it be great if everyone modeled the clothes they wore to school?

So, the next day I asked, "Who's next?"

They all looked at me and it got very quiet. Then, at the back of the room, a hand went up. A boy got out of his chair and began to recite, "The shoes are from Nike, and the pants are from The Gap." It was great!

The entire class got into the spirit of it and paraded down our makeshift aisle, music and all.

No one cared about how they looked; it was just fun to show off a bit and not be judged by anyone. So, go ahead! Take a closer look. Have a fashion show in your head. Who cares?

"Success is liking yourself, liking what you do, and liking how you do it."

—Maya Angelou

"When I dare to be powerful – to use my strength in the service of my vision, then it becomes less and less important whether I am afraid."

—Audre Lorde

STRENGTHS AND WEAKNESSES

IF YOU ARE GOING TO IMPROVE YOURSELF, you should know your strengths and be able to build upon them. In this exercise, I want you to list your strengths and weaknesses.

Strengths

1. _____

2. _____

3. _____

4. _____

5. _____

6. _____

Weaknesses

1. _____

2. _____

3. _____

4. _____

5. _____

6. _____

Get with a close friend and discuss your strengths as well as some possible ways that you might work on reducing your weaknesses.

Now, if something is suggested that you don't like, but you agree with, don't expend energy thinking about the fault. Instead, focus your energy to evaluate and possibly change it.

What you think of yourself is much more important than what others think of you.

RISK TAKING

The next portion of self-esteem deals with risk taking. Risk is a key factor in leadership. I want you and your friend to do something positive for someone else. Look how you can make their day!!

Jot down your risk.

KEEP IT POSITIVE!!

1. Together make a new friend.

2. _____

3. _____

4. _____

5. _____

**"Things work out best for those who make
the best of how things work out."**

—John Wooden

MAKING MISTAKES

From time to time as we go through life, we will make
mistakes. Some will be small, some big; some will be right,
some wrong. But what's really important is how we choose to
handle these situations. We will never be perfect in life, and
we must come to realize that mistakes are part of everyday life.
Don't ever believe your self-worth is gone when you make a
mistake. Not at all.

YOU'RE HUMAN. STRIVE FOR EXCELLENCE –
FORGET ABOUT PERFECTION.

Give yourself the right to be wrong!

**"To live a creative life, we must lose
our fear of being wrong."**

—Anonymous

CHRISTMAS **EVERY DAY**

I believe the MORE YOU DO FOR OTHERS, THE BETTER YOU
WILL FEEL. A good example of this feeling is Christmas,
Kwanzaa, Hanukkah, or any holiday where you give of yourself
to others. The key is giving without expecting something in
return. If you can do something for someone one day a week,
without expecting something in return, it has to make you feel
good. Let's start a good habit.

HERE ARE SOME EXAMPLES:

PARENTS:

Okay, here we go – starting with the people that made it
possible for us to be here. Do something for them that will just
freak 'em out!

1. Clean the house.

2. Clean your room.

3. Make dinner.

4. Buy them a nice card.

5. Be nice to your brother or sister.

And resolve to keep it going! I will do the following:

1. I will...

2. I will...

3. I will...

After you finish with your parents, maybe you can blow a
teacher's mind!

TEACHERS:

As a classroom teacher, I know what I'd freak out about. A huge
hurdle for students is understanding teachers are people too.

Trust me, we are. And we like compliments, too!

Here are a few ideas:

1. Invite a teacher over for dinner.

2. If you enjoyed their class that day, tell them.

The main thing you might want to be concerned about is your motive. So remember, you're doing this for their sake, not yours, without expecting anything in return!

FINALLY, LET'S DO SOMETHING FOR THE COMMUNITY.

Occasionally, and usually during the holiday season, we hear stories about a soup kitchen serving meals to needy families or homeless people seeking food, clothing, etc. I've taken students to the soup kitchen to work – you got it right, work – or better yet, to give. Get a few friends together, contact an area soup kitchen, ask an adult to join you, and go and make someone's day a little brighter. Take some food, help prepare it, serve it, and then eat with them. Meet someone new. Don't judge; just accept and appreciate them for who they are. Some other examples could be to help at a senior citizens home or center for disadvantaged youth.

I realize that in order to do any of these things you will need to take some risks, and maybe for some of you it might be a lot of risks. That's okay, be prepared. Some people might not be appreciative – that's okay, too. The key point is, how did YOU make someone feel?

"Success is...knowing your purpose in life, growing to reach your maximum potential, and sowing seeds that benefit others."

—John C. Maxwell

FOCUSING ON YOUR POTENTIAL

We've spent time on your strengths and weaknesses, now let's look a bit more closely. Was it easier for you to list your strengths or weaknesses? My bet is that you spent more time on your weaknesses. If I'm wrong, great; you'll have a good start to this next section.

As I mentioned earlier, this book won't fill you with false hope about how you can do anything you choose – let's get real! Basically, that is a set up.

If you set unrealistic dreams that exceed your limitations, you set yourself up for failure.

EXCEPT YOU CAN SET YOURSELF UP FOR SUCCESS. Psychologists have been quoted as saying that people seldom use more than 25% of their potential – that leaves 75% unused! Think of the possibilities! How much of his potential did Albert Einstein use? I wonder how much you use – 2%? 7%? I've said this countless times:

"Spend positive time and positive energy on what you can accomplish, not on what you cannot."

At times, we all play the comparison game. Consciously or unconsciously, we do it. When someone passes us in the hall or on the street, we give them the old once-up-and-down look – you know, starting from the shoes, we check them out all the way up to the head. The bad part is that we are setting ourselves up for disappointment again, because if the person exceeds our expectations, if we feel they are similar or even better in some way, there goes our self-esteem.

The best way to avoid this is not to play the game.

Geneticists say that the odds of our parents having another child like us are 1 in 102,000,000,000. We are not all the same, so let's face that fact and accept that we are special and different. You are unique. We're all unique.

Well, there you have it. Before going on to the next section, realize that you cannot be "self-esteemed" in all settings or after one reading. Go out, work at it, and make it happen...daily!

"Motivation is what gets you started. Habit is what keeps you going."

—Jim Ryun

SELF-ESTEEM POINTS TO REMEMBER

1. Feel good about how you perceive yourself.

2. Accept yourself for who you are – do not compare.

3. Do not take for granted your strengths and natural abilities.

4. If you do something well, build on that strength.

5. Ask questions, listen to what you hear, and learn from it.

6. Observe people you admire.

7. Believe in your potential and understand your limitations.

As you end each section, you will be provided with several pages in order to respond to questions that relate to each area of focus.

Look at these questions as a way to discover more about yourself. After all, this is all about you, so allow yourself to take the path of growth.

Hint: There are no correct or incorrect answers, only honest and dishonest ones.

1. I like myself most when I...

_____

_____

_____

_____

_____

_____

_____

_____

_____

_____

_____

_____

_____

_____

_____

_____

_____

_____

_____

**"You must expect great things of yourself
before you can do them."**

—Michael Jordan

2. A perfect day for me would be...

_____

_____

_____

_____

_____

_____

_____

_____

_____

_____

_____

_____

_____

_____

_____

_____

_____

"To accomplish great things, we must not only act, but also dream, not only plan, but also believe."

—Anatole France

3. The last time I really made someone feel good was...

_____

_____

_____

_____

_____

_____

_____

_____

_____

_____

_____

_____

_____

_____

_____

_____

_____

_____

_____

_____

**"If you really want to do something, you'll find a way;
if you don't, you'll find an excuse."**

4. It made me feel...(describe)

_____

_____

_____

_____

_____

_____

_____

_____

_____

_____

_____

_____

_____

_____

_____

_____

_____

_____

**"Success is walking from failure to failure
with no loss of enthusiasm."**

—Winston Churchill

5. The quality I wish I possessed...*(tell what and why)*

_____

_____

_____

_____

_____

_____

_____

_____

_____

_____

_____

_____

_____

_____

_____

_____

_____

_____

"The best way to cheer yourself up is to cheer someone else up."

—Mark Twain

6. My positive habits are...

_____

_____

_____

_____

_____

_____

_____

_____

_____

_____

_____

_____

_____

_____

_____

_____

_____

_____

_____

"Have confidence that if you have done a little thing well, you can do a bigger thing well, too."

—Storey

Before moving on to **Service Learning**, ask yourself the question, *"Have I fully completed this section to the best of my ability?"*

IF YES, PROCEED; IF NO, FINISH IT!

Nothing great was ever achieved without enthusiasm.

Every journey begins with a single step.

Happiness is an inside job.

**How high I am, how much I see,
how far I reach, depends on me.**

Improvement counts, no matter how small.

SERVICE LEARNING

This term may be new to you, but chances are you have participated in a service-learning project at some time during your school career. If not, after finishing this chapter, you can chalk up another valuable new experience.

I define "service learning" as integrating the accomplishment of a public task with conscious educational growth.

Through service-learning programs, if you choose to participate, you will be given an opportunity to link study with direct experience.

It is expected that you will want to learn about significant social issues, and I suggest investigating the historical, cultural, and political contexts of the need or issue to solidify your overall service-learning experience.

In 1980, I had a most unique opportunity. I was selected to travel with the international educational organization, *Up with People*.

If you're not familiar with *Up with People*, this nonprofit organization had the goal of building bridges of communication and understanding between diverse cultures of the world through two-hour musical performances and service-learning efforts.

Here's what it did for me: After a year of traveling and performing in over eighty different cities throughout the United States and Europe, what plays an important role in my life to this day is the emphasis on service-learning projects.

Both individually and with students I have worked on projects that include serving in community soup kitchens, spending a day with a senior citizen, volunteering at the Special Olympics and more. More than feeling good, these activities are good.

With each opportunity, I found a greater sense of concern for each project I got involved with. I found myself saying, *I wish I'd been doing this when I was younger*, but then I realized that it's never too late to get started!

So, what can you do?

We all have a skill, a gift, or a passion for something. It might be listening, working with animals, writing, teaching, typing, storytelling, tree planting, baking, organizing, office work, photography, computer work, or what have you.

The challenge I make to you is to prepare a service-learning project. Make a difference; you really can. And as you plan to get involved with the community, you may want to ask the following questions:

1a. What population do I want to work with (young, old, homeless, physically or mentally challenged)?

1b. Focus Area: _____

_____

_____

2a. How much time do I want to invest per week?

2b. Time: _____

_____

_____

3a. In exactly what area do I want to focus (social issues, i.e., soup kitchen; or service, i.e., day care)?

3b. Area: _____

_____

_____

"If you want to make a permanent change, stop focusing on the size of your problems and start focusing on the size of you!"

—T. Harv Eker

Now that you have narrowed down your choice of where you would like to do your community service project, your next step centers on finding an organization. Your community may have a United Way agency that can give you a list of resources.

After a careful investigation of the list, pick two or three organizations of interest to you. After doing that, call and set up an appointment for a visit.

A site visit will help you decide if the agency is a good fit for you. And if it is, you're on your way to becoming an active citizen working to benefit your community. That's something to feel good about and be proud of.

> **"If you don't design your own life plan, chances are you'll fall into someone else's plan. And guess what they have planned for you? Not much."**
>
> —Jim Rohn

You think you're done, right? Well, there is one more step:

That step: assessment!

Ask yourself the following questions:

1. What have I accomplished?
2. Did my experience meet my expectations?
3. What would I do differently?
4. Why was this important to me?
5. Could I have given more of myself?
6. What did I gain from the experience?
7. How can I apply this to my daily life?

Now you are complete. Remember, the more you give of yourself in an unconditional way, the better you will feel about yourself.

Take these tools and tell a friend.

> **We see possibilities in others, but do we ever dream of the possibilities within ourselves?**

MOTIVATION

Maybe you've said it yourself, or have heard it from someone else: If I were just a bit more motivated to do the things I want to do, I would have no problems at all.

We all have some great ideas, but the real issue is being able to follow through on them. The truth is if you don't have a plan to achieve your goals, you are lost.

In this part of *No Negatives* you will explore the art of goal setting and how it can benefit you.

I KNOW YOU'VE HEARD THE OLD PHRASE ACTIONS SPEAK LOUDER THAN WORDS.

FOR THIS SECTION TO BE BENEFICIAL TO YOU, ACTION MUST PREVAIL!!!

DREAM LIST

Just as Martin Luther King dreamed of civil rights responsibilities in the 1960s, for you to achieve your desired goals you must create a dream list.

I want you to complete a short dream list that includes the following areas:

1. Things to Learn:

I would like to learn how to...

_____

_____

_____

_____

_____

_____

_____

_____

_____

_____

2. Types of People to Meet:

I would like to meet the type of people who are...

_____

_____

_____

_____

_____

_____

_____

_____

_____

_____

3. Three Positive Unusual Tasks:

I would like to accomplish...

_____

_____

_____

_____

_____

_____

_____

_____

> **"You measure the size of the accomplishment by the obstacles you had to overcome to reach your goals."**
>
> —Booker T. Washington

Grab on to these dreams – when you do, you're on your way to turning them into reality.

THINGS I KNOW I CAN DO WELL

I realize society does not accept our saying in public what we think we are good at, but it's a free country and we can still do (almost) anything in a positive way that we wish. Sometimes we become the victim of judgmental behavior, as others assume we are conceited/stuck-up, but that's not what this is about – not at all. Here's your opportunity to list all the things you think you would be great at.

I think I would be great at...

1. _____

2. _____

3. _____

4. _____

5. _____

6. _____

7. _____

8. _____

9. _____

10. _____

NOW, HOLD ON TO YOUR TOP TEN. THEY WILL REALLY HELP YOU CHOOSE GOALS.

> **"People often say that motivation doesn't last.
> Well, neither does bathing – that's why
> we recommend it daily."**
>
> —Zig Ziglar

GOAL SETTING

Motivation and goal setting go hand in hand. If you are not motivated and organized with a purposeful plan, your goals will have no direction or final outcome. Here is a story of a man who had lofty goals. Yet, he believed, and conceived, and by acting and believing, he achieved them.

Dr. Daniel Hale Williams, an African-American, was born in the mid 1800s in the midst of racial unrest throughout our nation. Because of his positive motivation, Williams applied to and was accepted at Northwestern University in 1883. In 1891, he founded Provident Hospital in Chicago, Illinois, where he served as staff surgeon until 1912. He provided training for black interns and nurses at a time when they had difficulty obtaining medical training in other hospitals. By believing in his goals and following through with his dreams, Dr. Daniel Hale Williams was the first man to successfully complete open heart surgery in 1893.

As young people, you often hear from your parents that you should get off your *##!*!! and clean your room. Then, if it's not your parents, it's your teachers that want you to be motivated.

Have you ever thought that you would be more motivated if you were better organized, or better yet, if someone taught you how to be organized?

This is precisely what goal setting is all about.

NOW I'LL IDENTIFY THE THREE TYPES OF GOALS AND YOU'LL BE ON YOUR WAY.

"The reason most people never reach their goals is that they don't define them, or ever seriously consider them as believable or achievable. Winners can tell you where they are going, what they plan to do along the way, and who will be sharing the adventure with them."

—Denis Watiley

As mentioned previously, setting goals can help you get organized and provide a purpose and direction to your life's activities. Establish the habit of setting a goal for most everything you do, even those more unpleasant activities like cleaning your room and finishing your homework.

In order for goals to work in your favor, outline three different levels of goals:

1. Short Range.

2. Medium Range.

3. Long Range.

SHORT-RANGE GOALS are confidence builders.

You can reach them daily, weekly, or monthly. For example, keeping your room clean for one week straight. As you begin to set goals, don't be discouraged if you fall short of achieving goals within the time line you have allowed. It takes practice to learn how to adjust for the time needed.

Sample goal: I will keep my room clean this week.

MEDIUM-RANGE GOALS take anywhere from a few months to a year.

For example, if you are taking judo lessons, you master different levels like white, green, brown, and black belts. Your green belt might be a medium-range goal. Achieving any goal requires hard, consistent work. Don't let the length of time needed to reach these goals deter you from trying.

Sample g oal: I will maintain a B average this quarter.

LONG-RANGE GOALS are farther in the future.

Sometimes they scare people off, but don't let them. These goals are in the foreseeable future, but are worthy long-term projects. In your case, a good long-range goal could take anywhere from six months to a year.

Sample goal: I will practice piano four days a week for eight months.

Ironically, and here's the good news, in some ways long-range goals are the least threatening because you have more time to accomplish them!

1. **Set goals that will challenge you.** If you are challenged you will be forced to work harder. No pain, no gain!

2. **Set attainable goals.** Be realistic. Almost any goal can be reached, but you must allow for the time it takes to properly prepare yourself adequately. Goals must be set and achieved in a realistic order. In order to walk, you first have to crawl.

3. **Continue to strive.** After you have achieved some of your goals, continue to set new more challenging and rewarding ones. Do not settle for second best. Remember, you are trying to be the best person you can possibly be. You'll achieve that by setting higher goals.

4. **Believe in yourself.** Seek out friends and family that will support you. Sometimes goal achievement is a long, tough process, but take the long view and do not give up! Don't set goals that you hope to achieve – set goals you will achieve.

5. **Set your *own* goals.** Don't be so influenced that you are not doing what you want to do.

6. **Expect to reach your goals**. Think *Yes I can*, not, *No I can't*.

7. **Visualize your goals**. See them happen.

8. **Make a record** of your goals.

9. **Re-evaluate your goals.** Before completing your goals, give them another glance to see if they are within reach. You may need to modify the goals or stretch to achieve them in the time you have set.

10. **Reward yourself.** Plan ahead for celebration. Have it be another positive step...not something that will undo what you have just accomplished!

"There is no chance, no destiny, no fate, that can hinder or control the firm resolve of a determined soul."

—Ella Wheeler Wilcox

Keep trying. It is usually the last key on the ring that opens the lock.

Below, you have been provided an area designated for your short-, medium- and long-range goals. As you can see, the goal charts have been divided into four areas: **personal, family, school,** and **other**.

As you begin formulating your goals, use these charts as a starting point.

Short-Range Goals	**Date Completed**
Personal:	
Family:	
School:	
Other:	

Medium-Range Goals	**Date Completed**

Personal:

Family:

School:

Other:

Long-Range Goals   **Date Completed**

Personal:

_____

Family:

_____

School:

_____

Other:

_____

OBSTACLES: PLAN B

Remember that even the best laid plans in life have the real
possibility of running wild, so be aware that you may well
encounter obstacles in the pursuit of your goals. Learn to be

flexible and create other means of achieving what you have set out to do. If you have the ability to develop a "Plan B," you will have better success with goal setting.

Pick a goal that you have set for yourself. Now, take a moment to think about some possible obstacles you may encounter.

1. List obstacles:

    a. _____

    b. _____

    c. _____

Now, develop an alternative plan that could be used to achieve your goal.

2. Plan B:

    a. _____

    b. _____

    c. _____

This process can be duplicated with any and all of the goals you have set.

Everyone encounters barriers from time to time; even some of the most impressive and powerful leaders of our country. Don't allow obstacles to discourage you from pursuing your goals.

Few people remember, but many would be impressed by the track record of one of America's greatest heroes.

In 1832, he lost his job and then was defeated in a race for the state legislature in 1834. In 1835, a close female companion died, and in 1836, he suffered a nervous breakdown. He lost two more campaigns in 1838 and 1843 before a successful one for Congress in 1846. But he lost his bid for re-election in 1848. Then he ran for Senate in 1854 and in 1858 and lost both times, and was defeated as a nominee for Vice President in 1856.

But we all remember that in 1860, Abraham Lincoln was elected President.

The point should be clear: Mistakes and temporary setbacks hamper everyone. You can't let yourself worry about making mistakes, and you cannot allow them to get you down after you make them. A temporary setback is far different from utter failure. You haven't failed, you can't fail, until you accept defeat as permanent and stop trying; that is, you have not failed unless you quit.

Instead of despairing because of your mistakes, learn from them.

We learn best by trial and error. We try, fail, make adjustments, and try again.

Few worthwhile achievements – such as a great invention, a new theory – are accomplished in one try; we compensate for our mistakes, "we weed out the bugs" until we succeed. Learn to evaluate your errors and setbacks.

Ask yourself...

1. How did I fail?
2. How can I avoid making the same mistake again?

Convert mistakes and setbacks into the stepping stones of your progress.

Remember, you learn as much – or even more – from them than you learn from your victories.

VISUALIZATION

Visualization is a process that involves mind over matter.

The development of images in your mind will help you see how to turn a dream into reality. It's almost like a dress rehearsal before a performance. By first creating a positive situation in thought, making it a reality will be easier. Sometimes if you feel you have already done something, to do it again is less difficult. Practice makes perfect.

Goal setting and visualization go hand in hand. With a goal in mind, begin to imagine how, when, why, and where you'll turn this goal into a reality.

VISUALIZE BY:

1. Putting yourself into a relaxing environment and getting comfortable.

2. Picking a goal that you want to visualize.

3. Creating a thought process that will enable you to achieve your goal.

4. Asking yourself: *Is there a beginning, middle, and end in order for my goal to be reached?*

5. Making your visualization process as realistic as possible, and using as many of your senses as you can.

6. Practicing as you awaken, or better yet, just before you go to sleep.

MAPPING

Mapping is an activity that requires the use of the visualization process. Basically, mapping is an actual physical picture of a goal that you want to accomplish. It traces, step-by-step, your path toward achieving your goal. Visualization occurs when you *think* and *see* the kinds of things that you will include on your map.

Your map will be a kind collage; a composite of pictures and quotes cut from magazines and newspapers. It might also include pictures you have drawn and small items that relate to your goal and have special sentimental value, i.e., ticket stubs, pictures, cards, etc.

GUIDELINES FOR MAKING YOUR MAP:

1. Do a map for a single goal or area in which you are working.

2. Get a good-sized piece of cardboard paper.

3. Use lots of color.

4. Include a picture of yourself.

Occasionally the "I can't" syndrome gets hold of your thought process. You hit a dead end and want to give up. For this book to work effectively, you must become aware of how to fight and overcome it.

AFFIRMATION

A simple method called *affirmation* will help you stay on track so you can successfully accomplish your goals. To affirm means to make firm, and affirming is a process to help you remove self-doubt. An affirmation is a positive statement that indicates something is already so.

TO BE GOOD AT AFFIRMING YOU MUST PRACTICE – AND THEN PRACTICE SOME MORE. By practicing some positive affirmations five to ten minutes daily, I think that you will be surprised with the change in how you feel about yourself.

You'll begin to realize that you are an okay person with enough potential to accomplish what you set your mind to. Also, you'll be getting rid of some of your negative concepts about yourself. If you're willing to let it work for you, an affirmation will be one of the best friends you'll ever find.

Below are a few affirmations to help get you started:

1. **The more I commit to becoming a better person, the more it happens.**

2. **Meeting people is becoming easier for me.**

3. **I can accept people for who they are.**

4. **I am making others happy.**

5. **I am communicating more positively and more freely.**

KEY POINTS TO REMEMBER ABOUT AFFIRMATIONS

1. Phrase affirmations in the present tense, not in the future. Don't say, "I will get along with _____ better." Instead say, "I am getting along with _____ better."

2. When using affirmations, create a positive feeling within yourself that makes you believe it is actually happening. Don't doubt yourself.

3. Write short, simple affirmations.

4. Place each of your affirmations on a small 3x5 note card and position it in a location where you can be reminded of it, i.e., mirror, purse, wallet, locker, refrigerator, etc.

5. Once you are organized, you will be well on your way to making a positive impact on your friends, family, school and community. Use your potential to set goals, and above all, approach life with this philosophy: **If it is to be, it is up to me.**

1. If I could travel anywhere in the world, I would go to:

_____

_____

_____

_____

_____

_____

_____

Why?

_____

_____

_____

_____

_____

_____

_____

_____

_____

Don't be content with being average.
Average is as close to the bottom as it is to the top.

2. If you would receive $25,000 by doing a service-learning project in three months, what would it be?

_____

_____

_____

_____

_____

_____

_____

_____

_____

_____

_____

_____

_____

_____

_____

_____

_____

_____

_____

_____

_____

3. What is your project?

_____

_____

_____

_____

_____

_____

_____

_____

_____

_____

_____

How will you motivate others to do it?

_____

_____

_____

_____

_____

_____

_____

_____

_____

_____

_____

_____

4. In order to receive a passing grade in a class, you must interview three leaders.

Who will you interview? Why?

_____

_____

_____

_____

_____

_____

_____

_____

What five questions will you ask them?

1. _____

_____

2. _____

_____

3. _____

_____

4. _____

_____

5. _____

_____

Before moving on to **Communication**, again ask yourself the question, *Have I fully completed this section to the best of my ability?*

IF YES, PROCEED; IF NO, FINISH IT!!

**Success is the DAILY progression toward
a worthwhile goal.**

**Aim at the sun. You may not reach it, but you will fly
higher than if you never aimed at all.**

**I am not concerned that you have fallen;
I am concerned that you will arise.**

COMMUNICATION

Effective communication deals with an area that seldom gets the attention it deserves, but it is just as important: LISTENING.

IF YOU ARE AN ATTENTIVE LISTENER, YOU'RE PROBABLY AN **EFFECTIVE COMMUNICATOR**. If you have problems listening to people and you often interrupt their conversation, then this section of *No Negatives: A Teen Guide to Leadership and Service* may be of help.

This section offers some important ideas about effective communication and listening. So sit back, relax, and enjoy.

"Don't raise your voice, improve your argument."

Anonymous

THE ART OF LISTENING

To have the patience, genuine concern, and the will to listen is an earned skill. It is nothing special that you are born with, rather it's a mindset you develop. The following steps are ways to improve your listening skills:

1. **Have the WILL to listen.** People want to be heard. Do not allow yourself to think someone is not interesting. We all have great stories.

2. **Do not just listen, COMPREHEND.** Ask yourself if you understood what was being said.

3. **Give POSITIVE CUES** to the person you are listening to. Smile, nod, and look them in the eye.

4. **EMPATHIZE with the speaker.** Put yourself in his or her shoes so that you can better understand the speaker's point of view.

5. **DON'T try to ANTICIPATE** what the speaker is going to say so you can interrupt with an opinion. Hear him or her out.

6. **ASK positive questions.**

7. **DON'T PREJUDGE the person** you are listening to by their appearance.

Now that you have a better idea of HOW to listen, let's put this newly acquired knowledge to the test.

In previous sections of this *Leadership Guide*, I've asked you to take a risk or two. Well, this section is no different.

1. In a safe situation, go out and meet a stranger. Pick an individual that you know absolutely nothing about. Introduce yourself and spend some time talking to him or her. You may even want to show them this book. Try to make their day more pleasant or let them improve yours.

2. During lunch you notice someone eating alone. Go and join them or ask them to join your group.

3. There is a particular person you've really never gotten along with, but down deep you know if you try, you can get along with him or her. Make the extra effort to be kind and cooperative.

4. Create your own situation where you have to take the first step in communication.

NOT LONG AGO I HEARD A STORY ABOUT A LONELY AND DESPERATE GIRL. She didn't feel as though she fit in. She didn't have many friends, but one day she decided to go for a walk to see how many people would simply greet her with a "Hello."

Unfortunately in her pocket was a note that simply stated, "If I walk from my apartment to the pier and nobody speaks to me, I will jump."

The note was found on her body. Now, I don't know if we can lay the blame on anyone, but it makes you think.

You never know how you affect people – a simple hello never hurts!

**"The meaning of life is to find your gift.
The purpose of life is to give it away."**

—Anonymous

JUST ASK

During my first years as a teacher, I had the wonderful opportunity to coach basketball and track. One year I was coaching girls' track and we had a super team. We won the majority of our meets, and quite a few girls qualified for the state meet.

One girl in particular had done very well, finishing third in the 400-meter run. I was so happy for her because it was her first year on the team. Then I got wondering why she had not gone out for the team in previous years.

So I asked her, "Why didn't you compete before?"

She looked at me in a very reserved manner and simply stated, "No one asked me!"

Needless to say, I learned a good lesson that day: **You never know unless you ask!**

> **"Don't be afraid to give up the good to go for the great."**
>
> —John D. Rockefeller

Judging:

Inevitably judging is something we all do at times. I suppose we feel the need to label something good or bad.

The following is a list of suggestions I've compiled to give you some ideas to maintain a more positive COMMUNICATION environment.

1. **Try not to prejudge.** Do not judge a book by its cover! If you have ill feelings toward someone or something, get in touch with the real reasons for these feelings. Ask yourself, *do I feel this way for a GOOD reason or just because I don't like the way they look?* We all prejudge at times. Work on minimizing these times.

2. **Do not let others control your actions.** Be yourself! Be in control of your feelings and beliefs.

3. **Find good in others.** Too much time is spent on the negatives.

4. **Practice patience with others.** Make allowances for their differences and weaknesses. No two people are alike, so it's

far better to accept and appreciate their unique qualities.

5. **Learn to like and understand who or what you think is undesirable.** The unpopular, the loner, the sloppy dresser, the plain Jane or Joe. Everyone has something good to offer and popularity is fleeting. Most people are worth getting to know.

6. **Deal with the facts.** Insensitive moments often result from ignorance. Misunderstandings often occur because someone does not know all the facts.

7. **Listen to your language.** Be aware of what you say. "Hate" is a word often overused. Avoid it. "Boring" is just a state of mind that you allow yourself to be a part of.

8. **Empathize.** Begin to put yourself in the other person's shoes. Try to imagine his or her feelings at the time when you might be most critical of them.

NOW, GO OUT AND PRACTICE BEING MORE AWARE.

"Success does not consist in never making mistakes but in never making the same one a second time."

—George Bernard Shaw

1. You got into a heated discussion with a close friend. You depart not speaking, but later realize you were wrong. What do you do?

SOLUTIONS

1. _____
   _____
   _____
   _____

2. _____
   _____
   _____
   _____

3. _____
   _____
   _____
   _____

4. _____
   _____
   _____
   _____

5. _____
   _____
   _____
   _____

2. You have the opportunity to meet anyone in the world.

   a. Who will it be?

   _____

   _____

   _____

   _____

   _____

   _____

   _____

   b. What questions will you ask?

   _____

   _____

   _____

   _____

   _____

   _____

   _____

   _____

   _____

   _____

**An open mind affords the opportunity of dropping
a worthwhile thought into it.**

3. What is the biggest risk you have taken involving communication?

_____

_____

_____

_____

_____

_____

_____

_____

_____

_____

_____

_____

_____

_____

_____

_____

_____

_____

The price of excellence is discipline. The cost of mediocrity is disappointment.

4. Who have you (positively) impacted the most in your life?

_____

_____

_____

_____

_____

_____

_____

_____

a. How can you multiply this list?

_____

_____

_____

_____

_____

_____

_____

_____

_____

_____

_____

_____

For every problem, there is an opportunity.

5. In order for people to communicate more effectively, they need to:

_____

_____

_____

_____

_____

_____

_____

_____

_____

_____

_____

_____

_____

_____

_____

_____

_____

_____

_____

Attitudes are contagious. Make yours worth catching.

Before you go on to **Health**, ask yourself, *Have I fully completed this section to the best of my ability?*

AS BEFORE, IF YES, PROCEED; IF NOT, FINISH IT!!!!

**"To profit from good advice requires
more wisdom than to give it."**

—John Churton Collins

**Seek out new things, new people, and places
to expand the horizons of your world.**

HEALTH

HEALTH – IT'S A LOT MORE THAN NOT BEING SICK!

By Dr. Tim Houlton

Are you healthy? How do you know? Before we start to look at our state of health, we should define exactly what health is from Dorland's Medical Dictionary:

HEALTH: A state of optimal physical, mental, and social well-being, and not merely the absence of disease.

From this definition you can see that just because you don't have any symptoms of being sick (stuffy nose, headache, fever...), it doesn't necessarily mean you're healthy. Health is a state where you're in OPTIMAL SHAPE physically, mentally, and socially.

ILLNESS VS. WELLNESS

Have you ever thought about where good health comes from and what causes good health? Let's take an example. If you cut your finger, clean it, put a bandage on it, and wait a few days... and if you cut a piece of steak, clean it, put a bandage on it, and wait a few days, what's going to happen? Your finger will heal, but the steak won't change.

What's the difference? The steak has no life in it, but you are full of life, and THAT is what does the healing. The best doctor you'll ever find is already within your body, ready and willing to heal if you'll provide the right setting for it to happen.

Instead of focusing on what causes illness, let's take some time and look at what causes WELLNESS.

**"If you can't explain it simply,
you don't understand it well enough."**

—Albert Einstein

ILLNESS/WELLNESS CHART

You should notice a few things about the Illness/Wellness chart.

If you are at the point where you have no symptoms of being ill, it doesn't necessarily mean that you are on the wellness end of the chart. As you work on your physical, mental, and social well-being, you actually become HEALTHIER, and help PREVENT yourself from becoming sick. On the Wellness side of the chart, an arrow shows that as you work on improving your wellness, there's no limit to how great you can feel, and how healthy you can be.

**"Knowledge is being aware of what you can do.
Wisdom is knowing when not to do it."**

—Anonymous

PHYSICAL WELL-BEING

If you wear out your body, where are you going to live?

You only get one, and it has to last you a long time, so it's important to learn sooner, rather than later, how to take care of this wonderful human machine we have.

NUTRITION

If you plant corn, you don't get tomatoes.

Likewise, if you feed yourself junk food, you're not going to develop a strong, healthy body. Nutrients in the food you eat eventually transform into the tissues of your body, your hair, skin, bones, muscles, blood, nerves...so you can see that only by eating healthy foods can you develop and maintain a healthy body.

HEALTH TIPS

1. Eat more fresh fruit and vegetables, making sure to eat a variety of types, varieties, and colors.

2. Eat more whole grain and high-fiber foods. Examples are whole grain breads, oat bran, brown rice, dried beans, whole bran pasta, fresh vegetables, and fruits.

3. Drink 6-8 glasses of water each day. Your body is made up of 70% water, not 70% sodas, diet colas, and milkshakes. Natural fruit juices are okay, but cut back on the soft drinks and drink more water.

4. Eat a good breakfast. You can't be your best at school if you haven't had one. Yogurt, fruit, whole grain toast, juice, and whole grain cereals with milk are a great way to start the day.

5. AVOID JUNK FOOD! You don't want a junk body, so at least resolve to eat less of it! Try to limit or totally avoid pop, chocolate bars, candies, cakes, fried foods, fast foods, and any foods with preservatives and chemicals. Usually the ingredients on the label you never heard of and can't pronounce are to be avoided!

6. Avoid overeating and eating when you're upset, you're not hungry, or late at night.

> ## "You can do anything, but not everything."
>
> —Anonymous

EXERCISE

Here is one of my favorite stories about exercise and why it matters so much:

For the past several years, very few days have gone by in which I haven't seen an older man walking down the country road in front of my house. He wears an old fishing cap and is often carrying some bags.

I STOPPED TO TALK WITH HIM ONE DAY. I found that those bags were grocery bags and that he walked into town to pick up his groceries. That walk was over ten miles! To me, he looked like he was in his sixties. When I asked him how old he was, he answered, "I'm 84 years young!"

All of us should be so healthy when we're 84! Regular exercise is simply one of the most important health tools to use throughout your life.

See if you can list five different types of exercise you want to do.

1. _____

2. _____

3. _____

4. _____

5. _____

Regular exercise has many benefits. It's fun, challenging, can be relaxing, keeps your muscles strong and in good shape, promotes good circulation in your body, keeps your heart and lungs healthy and strong, and helps to prevent many types of illness. From walking to running or swimming, winning or having fun in sports, exercise helps you feel good about yourself and is something you can do any time, in any season, at any age. It will help you feel good and look great!

EXERCISE TIPS

1. Exercise at least 3-4 times per week...NO EXCUSES!

2. Before you exercise, take at least five minutes to stretch and warm up the muscles that you'll be using. It's also a good idea to stretch when you've finished exercising, to help your body cool down.

3. Remember **Fashion Show 101?** When you exercise, don't be concerned about how you look, how fast or slow you are, winning or losing...JUST HAVE FUN!

4. IF YOU DON'T USE IT, YOU'LL LOSE IT. If you don't exercise and use the muscles in your body, weakness and poor muscle tone will result. If you have weak muscles, the tendency is to develop bad posture.

5. On that subject, you should be very aware of your posture and that starts at school. Sit upright, and don't slump in your chair. Don't carry your books on the same side all of the time, instead switch arms regularly.

6. At home, avoid slumping over chairs or curling up on the sofa for hours to watch television.

7. Stay off the sides of your feet when you walk and don't sleep on your stomach. It puts a lot of stress on your neck and lower back.

Remember, **as the twig is bent, so grows the tree.** Keep a good posture when you sit, stand, and walk...and even sleep!

MENTAL WELL-BEING

Do you realize every thought and feeling you have directly affects your body? You can't separate the mental and the physical well-being...it's a total health picture. They work together.

Remember the night before your hardest test, or biggest game? Your heart was probably beating as fast as it does when you're exercising, but you hadn't moved. All of the thoughts and feelings you have affect your body. What's important in determining whether you move toward illness or wellness is your ATTITUDE. More than what happens to you, what really counts is your attitude and how you handle it.

It's commonly said that attitude creates action, so let's look at the following **Attitude Inventory** to find negative attitudes that can be converted to more positive attitudes, and move us toward the wellness end of the chart.

> **"You've got to get up every morning with determination if you're going to go to bed with satisfaction."**
>
> —George Lorimer

ATTITUDE INVENTORY

Negative/Uncreative Attitudes	Positive/Creative Attitudes
My life is full of problems	My life is full of challenges
Doctors are responsible for my health	Doctors may help, but I am responsible for my health
Complaining about what you don't have	Being thankful for what you do have
I have no symptoms, therefore I must be totally healthy	I can always improve my health by working on my physical, mental, and social well-being
I know how other people should behave	I accept other people for who they are
I look for the negative in every situation	I look for the positive in every situation
It's all a matter of luck	I get back what I put out
I'm afraid to do it	I'll do my best and go for it, regardless of the outcome
The glass is half empty	The glass is half full
That's not funny!	I never forget a sense of humor

HEALTH ACTION PLAN

I will make the following changes in my diet:

1. _____

2. _____

3. _____

4. _____

5. _____

The changes I would like to make in my exercise schedule, and new activities I would like to try are:

1. _____

2. _____

3. _____

4. _____

5. _____

Take your own personal **Attitude Inventory.** What are some of the attitudes you have that you would like to change?

Negative/Uncreative Attitudes   **Positive/Creative Attitudes**

_____

_____

_____

_____

_____

_____

_____

_____

_____

_____

_____

_____

You've learned a bit more about health and wellness, but remember:

**KNOWLEDGE IS POWER,
BUT ENTHUSIASM THROWS THE SWITCH.**

It's up to you. Be enthusiastic about improving your health. Take care of your body, but also your thoughts and feelings, attitudes, and relationships with others. You'll not only feel better and have less symptoms of illness, you'll experience new LEVELS OF WELLNESS.

HAVE FUN!

"I don't want to get to the end of my life and find that I lived just the length of it. I want to have lived the width of it as well."

—Diane Ackerman

LITERACY

THE IMPORTANCE OF READING AND WRITING

Literacy is having the reading, writing, speaking, listening, computing, and problem – solving skills to take advantage of the quality of life available to you. Quality of life is an umbrella term encompassing the degree of happiness you feel with your school, family, social, work, and spiritual life.. Literacy will enable you to seek and maintain a balanced quality of life that can only improve as you change and grow throughout your life.

YOUR ACADEMIC LIFE CENTERS ON BECOMING MORE LITERATE IN SPECIFIC AREAS.

Classes like Language Arts, Mathematics, Business/Consumer Studies, Science/Technology Studies, Performing Arts, Visual Arts, World Languages, Physical Education and Sports, Family Studies, and Social Studies offer information to increase your knowledge. Your ability to utilize or apply the knowledge in real life situations improves your quality of life.

To develop your academic literacy skills, pay attention to the study skills and learning suggestions your teachers give you. Teachers are expert learners in their content area and specifically developed their literacy skills in their subject areas to share their knowledge with students. Teachers want you to succeed, so if you are having trouble – just ask for help.

READING IS AT THE CORE OF ALL LITERACY SKILLS.

You may want to take a reading improvement course if it is a problem area. Your school will probably offer them or can give you information about local classes for you to attend. Improving your reading skills will be useful in almost all of your classes.

Another suggestion to improve your literacy skills in any specific subject is to ask a successful student for help. Ask them how they learn, how they study, and how they problem solve in class. Some students find it valuable to participate in self-formed study groups that meet outside of class time to review homework, study for tests, and do class projects.

You also will want to develop your personal literacy skills. These skills include being able to fill out job applications, balance your bank account, follow directions in completing projects, reading street signs and road maps, reading medicine labels, understanding credit agreements, reading advertisements, and honing other skills needed for functioning in your daily life.

Many of these personal literacy skills are called "survival" literacy skills because they are needed to survive in society today.

"Real difficulties can be overcome; it is only the imaginary ones that are unconquerable."

—Theodore N. Vail

Many people make their living providing literacy skills for other people. For example, accountants and tax experts help people less literate to prepare their income taxes each year. Lawyers read and write for people who do not know or do not want to take the time to read or write their own agreements.

YOU CAN BECOME MORE PERSONALLY LITERATE BY ASKING YOUR PARENTS OR ANOTHER PERSON TO SERVE AS A MENTOR.

You may want to get several mentors to help you with all of the literacy skills you want to learn, such as how to read and understand certain information, how to understand when you hear information, and how to speak about that information. Practice acquiring and using the information until you feel comfortable with your ability to function in the problem area. As you work on becoming literate, you may make a few mistakes. That's okay! Mistakes tell you what you need to work on next. Your library can also recommend books that might help you.

One great way to increase your own literacy skills is to help others increase theirs! People of all ages, from toddlers to teens and adults – need help and are eager to learn. Reading is one of the greatest areas of need in literacy programs. Reading to children is important in helping those children learn to read, even if they won't be reading on their own for a few years yet. There are many adults who also need help learning to read. You can volunteer through your school, local library, or literacy agency.

If you are literate in a subject (knowledgeable and able to use and share information), you may want to help someone else become more literate in that area. This will help solidify your skills, too.

Ask your teacher if you can become a peer tutor. Community agencies may also have need of tutors for their adult training programs. You will be offered training on how best to work with the people in the programs.

An opportunity for assisting other people in literacy programs is available to students in colleges and universities. The Student Literacy Corps is a program funded by the United States Department of Education. It establishes a course or courses in community colleges and on university campuses, to educate undergraduate students in becoming tutors of adults who lack literacy skills. The courses require that you tutor an adult while you are taking classes. You learn and practice at the same time. Everybody learns!

Literacy is just like any gift you receive. Unless you accept, unwrap, and use the gift, it's worthless. Knowledge alone is worthless unless it is accepted by you and used by you in real life situations. There are few people who cannot learn. If you lack literacy skills, go get help.

Commit to becoming literate and proficient in your academic and personal life. Your quality-of-life-umbrella will only be strengthened for it, and the work acquiring and using literacy skills pays off now and for the rest of your life. Increasing your literacy skills, or helping someone increase theirs, will boost your self-confidence. It's all part of being the best you can be.

There are also booklets available through the federal government and your local extension agency, that can give you tips to increase your literacy.

> **"Fortune sides with him who dares."**
>
> —Virgil

LITERACY ACTION PLAN

As you begin to develop a plan for HOW you are going to implement literacy into your daily life, ask yourself the four W's:

1. WHAT specifically am I going to do?

2. WHO will be involved in my literacy assignments?

3. WHEN will it take place?

4. WHERE will it be?

What:

Who:

When:

Where:

Good Luck!

TIME MANAGMENT

How many times have you heard your parents, teachers, or others say: "You are wasting your time!" You probably ask yourself, *What difference does it make what I do with my time?* After reading this section on time management, you will have a good feel for the importance of managing your time and how you'll benefit because of it.

We need to ask ourselves, "What value is there in managing our time? After all, isn't time something that we will always have?"

MANAGING OUR TIME WISELY ALLOWS US TO DO THREE THINGS:

1. Accomplish the tasks that we NEED to get done (i.e., go to school, finish papers, eat, sleep, clean room, etc.)

2. Have time for the things we WANT to do (i.e., go to a movie with friends, play sports, go to dances, read, shop, etc.)

3. Use time to plan ahead for the future (i.e., where you might want to go to college, where you can go on vacation, what you might buy for a friend's birthday, etc.)

Let's explore how well you manage your time. Ask yourself the following questions:

Do you ever analyze your daily routine to see where your time goes?

_____ yes _____ no

Do you have a system for keeping track of daily "things to do?"

_____ yes _____ no

Do you do your most important jobs first?

_____ yes _____ no

Do you use a weekly schedule?

_____ yes _____ no

Do you schedule time each day for rest, relaxation, and physical activity?

_____ yes _____ no

How did you do? Are you organized with your time and the tasks you need to do? If not, there is a quick and easy way you can help yourself. It will give you a sense of accomplishment at the end of your day.

TRY IT! YOU'LL LIKE IT!

**"Don't let what you cannot do interfere
with what you can do."**

—John R. Wooden

"TO DO" LIST

Make a DAILY "To Do" List.

I MUST DO	I SHOULD DO	I COULD DO
_____	_____	_____
_____	_____	_____
_____	_____	_____
_____	_____	_____
_____	_____	_____
_____	_____	_____
_____	_____	_____
_____	_____	_____
_____	_____	_____
_____	_____	_____
_____	_____	_____
_____	_____	_____
_____	_____	_____
_____	_____	_____
_____	_____	_____
_____	_____	_____

DO IT NOW! Procrastination only lends itself to frustration!

Now that you have a good grasp of how to prioritize the things you need to accomplish, let's look at the different strategies you can adopt to help you change your time management habits:

1. Don't try to do everything all at once.

2. Get someone else to help you – SUPPORT HELPS!

3. Don't get down on yourself if you slip up.

4. Reward yourself for the changes and progress you do make.

REMEMBER, IMPROVEMENTS IN YOUR TIME-MANAGEMENT SKILLS ARE THINGS ONLY YOU ARE LIKELY TO SEE!

DANGER: Following the above set of guidelines may be hazardous to your health, change your life, and result in more organized, smooth-sailing, fun-filled days!!

"People rarely succeed unless they have fun in what they are doing."

—Dale Carnegie

TIME MANAGEMENT TIPS

As you can see, managing your time can be fun and creative!

Dedicate time each morning to planning your daily tasks, and you'll find yourself saving time in the long run! It is a fact that more time is wasted by not being organized than by taking the initial time to plan your work!

TO STAY ORGANIZED AND ON TRACK, USE THESE TIME MANAGEMENT TIPS:

1. Keep an appointment book or a spiral notebook.

2. Write a "to do" list every day.

3. Maximize every spare minute.

4. Make the most of transition times.

5. Learn to say NO when appropriate and make sure you have enough time for yourself.

6. Control interruptions.

7. Wean yourself from too much television.

8. Concentrate on one thing at a time.

9. Develop procedures for routine matters.

10. Spend more time planning and challenge yourself to write things down, rather than just thinking about it and hoping you remember.

11. Ask the question, "What is the best use of my time right now?"

12. Don't be afraid to make mistakes; we learn many of the most important lessons from our mistakes.

13. Break tasks down into 15-30 minute intervals so you can utilize the little times in your day.

14. Don't spend any more time sleeping than what is needed.

15. Run as many errands as possible at one time.

16. Don't spread yourself too thin!

17. BUILD YOUR WILLPOWER: Time management is self-discipline!

Start learning to manage your time today and it will teach you good habits for the future! Some of the most successful people in this world are the ones who have mastered the art of time management. IT PAYS TO PLAN!

Good luck! YOU CAN DO IT!!

"Failure is the condiment that gives success its flavor."

—Truman Capote

MENTORING

Imagine having an older friend you could spend time with once a week or twice a month, who has all the wisdom and experience in life you WISHED you possessed.

THAT SCENARIO IS NOT OUT OF YOUR REACH. YOU JUST NEED TO FIND A MENTOR.

WHAT IS A MENTOR?

A mentor is a person who oversees the development and leadership path, through teaching, counseling, listening and providing overall support, to the mentee – that's you! Mentoring is a structured, enduring relationship between a young person and an adult, providing help, guidance, ,and support. The aim of mentoring is to develop in the young person the skills and self-confidence necessary for a fulfilling life.

Sound like something you would be interested in? Read on!

**"All progress takes place
outside the comfort zone."**

—Michael John Bobak

Next, we will look at the following two questions: "What can a good mentor do for me?" and "How can I find a mentor?"

A good mentor is a role model, friend, or teacher who...

...Supports, encourages and guides you.

...Helps you build your self-esteem.

...Listens carefully for feelings as well as content.

...Shares your aspirations and dreams.

...Helps you design realistic goals.

...Provides opportunities that fit your needs.

...Shows you how to be independent and responsible.

...Is a good motivator.

...**BELIEVES IN YOU!**

"The starting point of all achievement is desire."

—Napoleon Hill

HOW CAN YOU FIND A MENTOR? THAT'S EASY – JUST ASK!

Review the previous list and become familiar with what a mentor can do for you. You will need to narrow down the list to fit you. Don't be put off if you think you don't know someone with these qualities. They are out there!
Ask your parents to help.

Also, you might consider the following types of people as a mentor:

- Doctor
- Lawyer
- Teacher
- College Professor
- Nurse
- Entrepreneurs (look it up!)
- City Employees (Mayor, police, etc.)
- Performer
- Anyone you respect and admire

After you locate this person, you might have useful discussions about:

- Work, school, or home adjustment.
- Educational or career goals.
- Ways to communicate more effectively with friends and family.
- The mentor's place of employment; spend a day with him or her.

Spend time together: go to a movie, skiing, bike riding, shopping, eating, or just sitting and talking. These will be opportunities to get to know each other better and learn from each other.

As you can see, the choices are wide open. Don't limit the amount of fun you can have!

Finally, a few responsibilities of the mentee (that's you!):

1. **You should be time-conscious and respectful.**
   Keep all appointments you set with your mentor. If an appointment has to be cancelled, the mentor should be contacted. If a mentor cannot be reached on the phone, a message should be left.

2. **Be proactive; a mentee should initiate a meeting.**
   Even though a mentee is a student, a lot of the responsibility for the success of the relationship depends on the mentee.

GO OUT AND MAKE SOMEBODY'S DAY BY ASKING THEM TO BE YOUR MENTOR! THEY WILL BE HONORED.

"The only place where success comes before work is in the dictionary."

—Vidal Sassoon

PRE-COLLEGE COUNSELING

By Susan M. McGuire

Your College MindSet – It's Time to Get Ready!

College is just so far, far away. I mean, really – *college?* Maybe you have an older brother or sister that isn't even in college yet, so why should you be thinking about it?

Because too many students get to eleventh grade and wish they'd done more to prepare. What can you do? Recognize the value of planning for it now, and begin with paying attention to *you*.

Learn more about what you're good at!

Knowledge is power, and the more empowered you are, the greater your chances of being successful. Strong leadership skills will open doors for you in life, but imagine your impact upon others if you're also knowledgeable in what interests you most.

The most successful people in life eat, drink, and sleep their passions – and many began doing it at an early age – often outside of school in their free time. Here are a few examples:

Did you know Tiger Woods started playing golf at the age of 2? And tennis champions Venus and Serena Williams began to play at 10? Most professional tennis players began even earlier!

Bill Gates, founder of Microsoft and the world's wealthiest man, wrote his first program in eighth grade after being introduced to and fascinated by a strange new machine called a "computer."

Neil DeGrasse Tyson, the African-American astrophysicist and narrator of the "Cosmos" TV show, became interested in astronomy at age nine after visiting Hayden Planetarium in New York. He attended courses there during high school, earned a Bachelor's at Harvard, and a Ph.D. at the University of Texas, before later becoming director of the very planetarium that inspired his love of the stars.

And Alicia Keys, superstar singer, songwriter, and multiple Grammy winner, was exposed to music early. She began training in classical piano at seven, wrote her first songs at fourteen, and then graduated valedictorian of her class at the Professional Performing Arts School. She eventually earned admission to Columbia University.

Successful people have 3 things in common:

1. They discovered their interests at a young age.

2. They developed interests in their free time, outside of school, which...

3. Opened doors, allowing them to influence others doing what they loved.

I know what you're thinking: *I'm no Tiger Woods, Bill Gates, or Alicia Keys!*

You don't have to be! Most successful people aren't celebrities, but leaders in their professions who developed their interests at a young age. Everyone was born with the ability to be great at *something*, so get out there, try new things, and find yours.

Take advantage of opportunities inside *and* outside of school to learn something new. A new interest you're good at and passionate about will lead to amazing opportunities for you.

Sometimes in trying new things, you learn what you are *not* interested in, and that's okay, too! Piano lessons were okay three years ago, but now are downright painful. Fine. You learned what you *don't* want to do.

Maybe quitting piano meant time for an astronomy class, and you got turned on to black holes, nebulae, and outer space. You got hooked and became passionate about science!

What's most important is putting yourself out there to try and experience new things.

LISTEN FOR CLUES.

How do you discover your strengths and your special gifts? Listen to your teachers, parents, grandparents, siblings, friends, pastors, and rabbis – the people that really know you. If you *enjoy* what they're praising you for, and you're excited, happy, or flat-out fascinated with it, look for ways to do more and you're on your way.

A few examples:

IF YOU LIKE MATH AND YOUR TEACHER SAYS YOU'RE GOOD AT IT, ASK YOUR TEACHER TO TEACH YOU MORE CHALLENGING PROBLEMS AFTER SCHOOL. Or, ask your teacher if there's someplace you can go after school, in the summer, or on weekends to learn more about math. Ask a responsible adult to take you to your local community center and inquire about after school programs in math. Commit yourself!

If you like writing stories, and find yourself writing in your free time, ask your teachers if they'll read your work and give you feedback. Ask them if there are places where you can go after school, in the summer, or on weekends to learn more about writing. Find out what's going on at your local library. Visit the bookstore and take notice when a writer you like is coming to town. Go on the Internet and find out if there are online literary magazines for youth that you can submit your stories to. Remember in the last chapter when we talked about the importance of mentors? Ask a mentor if they can help you discover some enrichment opportunities for young people who like to write. This is how successful people get their start.

If you like singing, find ways to sing more.

Ask your teachers or parents if there are places where you can go after school, on weekends, or in the summer to develop your talent. Make a commitment to what you love.

NOW RUN AND GIVE THIS BOOK TO A PARENT. THE REST OF THIS CHAPTER IS FOR THEM.

PARENTS! THIS IS FOR YOU.

Middle school really *is* a critical time in your child's academic life. It is an invaluable opportunity to begin developing the leadership skills important to their success, and to learn how to help position your child for great college opportunities by the time they reach the twelfth grade.

Why now, in middle school? It's when kids make unconscious decisions about what kind of students they are going to be, now and in the years to come.

BE AN ACTIVE PARTICIPANT IN SHAPING YOUR SON OR DAUGHTER'S ACADEMIC CURRICULUM.

Think of yourself as a partner with the school guidance counselor. These remarkable people are called upon to balance many things, including attending to the academic needs of hundreds of students. Guidance counselors want to get to know each student personally – that's why they chose the profession – but their counseling caseload is often daunting. The ratio of students to counselor can be upwards of four hundred to one!

That's why your involvement is so crucial. You need to be your child's advocate, particularly when it comes to choosing the academic track most appropriate for them. Be sure you're comfortable with the curricular choices being made in the seventh and eighth grade, because these are their foundation years. The level of course work in these grades, particularly mathematics, often determines how far they'll get by junior and senior years of high school, directly impacting the colleges your child will be eligible to attend.

For example: If you have the opportunity to help your child advance in math as a seventh grader, do that. I have met students who happened to enjoy math and were motivated to do a little extra work outside of the normal school setting – with a willing teacher or at a local tutoring center, perhaps – advancing them well beyond their classmates. This not only creates a path for advanced study in high school, it also creates within that child the sense of accomplishment and self-confidence that comes from performing well within their area of strengths and gifts. And usually, it opens all kinds of doors for that child during high school, their college years, and throughout life.

As a high school guidance counselor and former admissions officer at a highly selective university, I learned that students who don't reach a certain level in mathematics (Pre-calculus or Calculus) are at a huge disadvantage in the admissions process, and usually ineligible for admission to top schools.

WHY MIDDLE SCHOOL IS CRUCIAL.

Middle school is the ideal time to get kids to advance within their areas of academic strength. And they're a captive audience: too young to drive, loads of free time, and less susceptible to the distractions of a high school student. Give them a constructive way to use their time and develop their strengths.

Set them up to take learning seriously. With a taste of accomplishment, they truly begin to soar.

So what's the lesson in all of this? Monitor decisions being made at school about your son or daughter's academic path. If you have question, get them answered. Be honest and realistic about their capabilities, but don't let anyone dumb down their education.

IN ADDITION TO ACADEMICS, PAY CLOSE ATTENTION TO THEIR DEVELOPING INTERESTS.

Every young person has strengths and gifts. Actively identify your child's developing strengths, even in areas that don't interest you. Don't confuse *your* priorities or interests with your child's!

You may wish you had continued with ballet in your youth, and then find yourself forcing your child to love this activity, which is actually quite excruciating for them. Or, maybe you have always loved sports but were never a good athlete, and you unconsciously try to make your poor, disinterested child love sports too.

Perhaps your son or daughter has an eye for art and draws whenever possible. Or perhaps he or she seems to have an ear for music, or is genuinely fascinated by the stars. Those are telling moments – do not casually pass them by!

BE RESOURCEFUL AND HELP THEM FIND WAYS OF DEVELOPING THOSE INTERESTS.

If your son or daughter is showing a particular interest, help feed it. Is your child fascinated by science? Fond of drawing? Obsessed with computers or crazy about chess? Encourage your child to find other ways of committing themselves to their interests. *It's the single most important thing you can do to jump start your child's academic success.*

If you can't identify an obvious strength or interest in your child, expose them to enrichment opportunities that broaden their perspectives with new ideas; they're likely to discover one.

THINK... SUMMERTIME!

Summer Matters – an enrichment program for middle schoolers in California, developed fun and educational summer enrichment programs that have improved literacy, reduced the chance of risky behavior, and increased overall self-confidence. In their words, "summer programs emphasizing both academic and social components lead to positive outcomes for students..."

The National Summer Learning Association, associated with Johns Hopkins University, is so convinced about the value of summer activities, they're holding programs across the country. For them, summer learning experiences "account for about two-thirds of the difference in the likelihood of pursuing a college preparatory path in high school."

Summer enrichment and out-of-school learning is an *essential* component of overall success for young people – particularly students in low-income communities. Helping your child identify and commit to their interests and strengths will propel them to being fully engaged during high school and affect the trajectory of their lives.

HOW ALL OF THIS RELATES TO COLLEGE ADMISSION.

In a recent *Forbes* magazine interview, the Dean of Admissions at a competitive university said top colleges look for evidence of two qualities in young people's lives: engagement and impact.

Colleges are looking for students who are fully engaged *academically* – challenging themselves with the most rigorous classes available – and fully engaged *outside of the classroom* – students committed to worthy interests where their passion emanates brilliantly.

Selective colleges are looking for students making an impact for the better of their schools *and* communities – the change-makers. Students whose commitment to their interests inspires their wanting to make a difference in the world around them.

More than the secrets of admission to the best colleges in America, the message is clear: When young people discover their interests and commit themselves to their passions, the world opens up to them in ways that neither they – nor you – could begin to imagine.

This is the best pre-college counseling advice you could possibly receive.

Knowing this, the time is *now*, in their middle school years, to position them to take advantage of the full array of college and scholarship opportunities that can be available to them.

A little homework to get *you* started:

Get a piece of paper and a pen, and take a little time to answer a few questions:

What is my son/daughter good at?

_____

_____

_____

_____

_____

_____

What does my son/daughter seem most drawn to?

_____

_____

_____

_____

What is my son/daughter doing when his or her eyes light up?

_____

_____

_____

_____

What type of activity is an energy-drainer for my son/daughter?

_____

_____

_____

_____

Is what I want my child to enjoy what they actually enjoy?

_____

_____

_____

_____

_____

HINDSIGHT IS 20/20.

It may seem some parents have the knack for giving their kids the best chances at college and in life, but don't be fooled. More often than not, they're the beneficiary of *hindsight* – either theirs someone else's.

Maybe they attended a top college or university or know someone who did, and learned what a young student needs to do to achieve high school and college success.

Perhaps they encountered knowledgeable, connected people that took an interest, opened doors, and offered insight into how best to prepare.

Still other parents, taking it upon themselves to become informed, read, researched, and figured it out. The more engaged and proactive parents are now, the more equipped they'll be to empower their children educationally throughout high school.

So I hope you're inspired by the stories of Venus and Serena Williams, Tiger Woods, Bill Gates, Neil deGrasse Tyson, and Alicia Keys. I included them for a reason.

ODDS ARE THEY HAD A PROACTIVE PARENT.
I HOPE YOU BECOME ONE.

Start today to create your action plan to help your child become the best they can be.

COPING WITH

STRESS

In today's world, you are exposed to obstacle after obstacle. How you handle these setbacks relates directly to the type of day-to-day life you choose to live.

IN THIS CHAPTER WE'LL FOCUS ON **EFFECTIVELY** COPING WITH STRESS BY ZEROING IN ON:

1. Decision making

2. School pressures

3. Family relationships

4. Friendships

5. Academic school pressures

In your own words, define stress:

_____

_____

_____

_____

_____

_____

_____

WHERE ARE YOU?

Read through all thirty statements and rate yourself as to how you typically feel or act in each situation.

1=never   2=seldom   3=sometimes   4=frequently   5=always

_____ 1. Meeting new friends is very stressful for me.

_____ 2. My friends think I study too much.

_____ 3. What happens in my life is determined by fate and circumstances.

_____ 4. If given the chance, I will work alone.

_____ 5. I'm anxious when my school assignments are not clearly laid out.

_____ 6. A bad grade makes me depressed for days.

_____ 7. I pride myself in finishing quickly and accurately.

_____ 8. Having to make decisions is particularly stressful for me.

_____ 9. There's little I can do to influence the decisions of those in authority.

_____ 10. My school work is less productive when interacting with others.

_____ 11. I rely more on other people's opinions than on my own.

_____ 12. I am a private person.

_____ 13. I usually work better with deadlines and time pressures.

_____ 14. It's impossible to change society, so I go along with the status quo.

_____ 15. I withdraw from people rather than confront them with problems.

_____ 16. If one method works, I'm not likely to change it.

_____ 17. I need the praise of others to feel I am doing a good job.

_____ 18. Since I do not want to fail, I avoid risk.

_____ 19. I seldom feel good about myself.

_____ 20. I become upset with changes in my routine.

_____ 21. I do not reveal things about myself.

_____ 22. I tend to become overly cautious and anxious in new situations.

_____ 23. I tend to produce more and more work in less time.

_____ 24. Because I am so busy at school, I seldom have time for myself.

_____ 25. If someone criticizes me, I begin to doubt myself.

_____ 26. I pride myself on being orderly, neat, and punctual.

_____ 27. I don't like to go to parties or places where there are a large number of people.

_____ 28. Luck has a great deal to do with success.

_____ 29. I do my studies while watching TV or talking on the phone.

_____ 30. I become upset if told I'm wrong.

If you scored between 30-45

This indicates that you possess characteristics which defuse much of the stress in your life. Qualities that make you a prime candidate for a leadership position since you function well under pressure.

If you scored between 46-75

This indicates that you generally have good control. It's not likely that your personality aggravates your reaction to stress.

You probably feel that you can handle and control most situations.

If you scored between 76-115

This reflects a good balance. You will have to make a conscious effort, however, to keep your behavior on the positive end of the scale when going through a stressful situation.

If you scored between 116-135

This indicates room for improvement. You may usually feel unable to handle high amounts of stress for prolonged periods of time.

If you scored between 136-150

Your personality possesses characteristics likely to generate a great deal of stress for you at school. Your personality creates much of its own stress and this may limit your ability to function well under pressure.

If you are not pleased with your standing, how can you change it? I urge you to create an action plan and to move forward with your decision.

SOLUTIONS FOR STRESS

To avoid some of the pitfalls of stress, incorporate the following ten suggestions into your way of doing things.

1. You aren't perfect; admit your mistake and get on with it.

2. If you fail at a task, you aren't a failure as a person! Use it as a learning experience and move on.

3. Increase your ability to deal with change; become more adaptable.

4. Learn to compete against yourself in relation to the needs of your environment. Quit worrying about the other person; it distracts you from your goals.

5. Relax and gain a little perspective; when you overreact with anger, sharp criticism, and defensiveness, you only hurt yourself.

6. Develop an inquiring mind. Get the facts; don't rely on others.

7. Learn to ask questions and listen to the answers.

8. Conflict typically arises when you and the other person don't understand one another or refuse to compromise. Be ready and willing to compromise.

9. Don't be indecisive or procrastinate. Be action-oriented; prioritize and then just do it.

10. Don't play the martyr. Life is too short.

DECISION MAKING

To avoid stress, think ahead and make a plan to address a problem or situation before things get out of hand.

Write down five important decisions you made recently.

1. _____

2. _____

3. _____

4. _____

5. _____

Now, review and respond to the following statements.

1. Identify the specific problem.

2. Describe the problem and your usual response to it in terms of who, what, where, when, how, and why.

3. Brainstorm possible solutions.

4. Look at the positive and negative consequences.

5. If your outcome is satisfactory, REWARD YOURSELF. If not, go back to the top of the list of brainstorming ideas and come up with more solutions.

If you have a problem:

State your problem

Outline your response

List your alternatives

View the consequences

Evaluate your results

SOLVE IT!

"The successful warrior is the average man, with laser-like focus."

—Bruce Lee

WORDS TO THE WISE

So wrapping up, control what you can, and don't fret over what you can't.

- **Control events**
  - Plan ahead
  - Set priorities
  - Don't spread yourself too thin

- **Control your attitude**
  - See the big picture...be positive
  - List stresses you CAN change and accept the rest: fix them or forget them
  - Shift from worry to problem solving

NOW, GO CHILL!!

> "In my experience, there is only one motivation,
> and that is desire. No reasons or principle
> contain it or stand against it."
>
> —Jane Smiley

SUMMARY

Now that you have successfully completed *No Negatives*, go and celebrate, and make someone's day.

As you continue to move through life, you will have many opportunities to utilize these principles daily. I urge you to do so in the most positive, productive way and make the most of every day.

Best of Luck,

J. Victor McGuire, Ph.D.

REMEMBER:

Whatever your mind can conceive and believe, it will achieve.

Just don't look back unless you want to go that way.

YOU ARE UNIQUE.

In all of history there was never anyone else exactly like you. And in all of infinity to come, there will never be another you.

FOR EVERY OBSTACLE THERE IS A SOLUTION.

Nothing in the world can take the place of persistence.

DO IT NOW.

THERE IS NO FAILURE EXCEPT IN NO LONGER TRYING.

YOU CAN ALWAYS BETTER YOUR BEST.

To accomplish great things, you must not only act, but also dream; not only plan, but also believe.

The greatest mistake, and the only fatal mistake, is giving up.

If you have built castles in the air, you need not be lost – put foundations under them.

SUCCESS IS AN ATTITUDE. GET YOURS RIGHT!

AUTHOR

A published author and a seasoned facilitator for over 30 years, Victor has been a public school teacher, school administrator, and professor at several universities. He has been to South Africa on a

Fulbright-Hays scholarship and traveled the world with Up with People.

Most importantly, Victor is at his best when he gets the opportunity to work with middle school students to help them truly activate their potential for the world that awaits them.

Made in the USA
Charleston, SC
12 February 2017